Freedom and Responsibility

Weaving the Threads of Dominican Spirituality

Dominicans Today

Freedom and Responsibility

Weaving the Threads of Dominican Spirituality

Cabra Collective

ATF PRESS

Adelaide 2017

This book has been a collective work with contributions by many people who are or were linked with Cabra Dominican College and its history. Hilary Regan coordinated the project and takes editorial responsibility for this volume. Others contributed by; working on the concept, bringing ideas to the project, providing quotes or pieces of writing, consulting on the project, working on the art work, photographs and lay-out, providing knowledge of the tradition, and by assisting with valuable proof-reading. These people include a core group of Cabra staff and others.

Cabra Collective: Patricia Cramp, Deborah Lubatti, Gabrielle Kelly OP, Margaret Kennedy OP, Bernadette Kiley OP, Angela Moloney OP, Hilary Regan, Brian Schumacher, Antonine Stagg, Helen Telford

National Library of Australia Cataloguing-in-Publication entry

Title: Freedom and Responsibility Weaving the Threads of Dominican Spirituality

ISBN:
978-1-925309-53-9 (paperback)
978-1-925309-54-6 (hardback)
978-1-925309-55-3 (epub)
978-1-925309-56-0 (kindle)
978-1-925309-57-7 (pdf)

ATF PRESS

An imprint of the ATF Ltd
PO Box 504 Hindmarsh
SA 5007
ABN 90 116 359 963
www.atfpress.com
Making a lasting imprint

Artworks provided by: Sheila Flynn OP, Kim En Jong OP, Mary Horn OP, Maurice Keating OP, Cristóbal Torres OP, Rosemary Yelland OP
Front Cover Artwork: Dominican Last Supper, Cristóbal Torres OP
Back Cover Artwork: St Dominic, Sheila Flynn OP

Graphic Design & Layout: Lydia Paton
Font (Body text): Garamond (12pt)

Table of Contents

Winter to Spring—seeking justice

January, February, March

Spring to Summer—celebrating community and diversity

April, May, June

8. Margaret of Castello 1287–1320 (April 13)

9. Catherine of Siena 1347–1380 (29 April)

10. Columba Boylan 1847–1910 (3 May)

11. Meister Eckhart 1260–1329 (14 May)

12. Luigia Tincani 1889–1976 (31 May)

13. Segrid Undset 1882–1949 (10 June)

14. Mechtild of Magdeburg 1208–1292/94

15. Lent

16. Easter

17. Pentecost

18. *Corpus Christi-* The Eucharist

Summer to Autumn—seeking truth

July, August, September

19. Bartolome de las Casas 1484–1566 (18 July)

20. Mary Magdalene (22 July)

21. Jane of Aza 1135–1205 (2 August)

22. Dominic de Guzman 1171–1221 (8 August)

23. Francisco de Vitoria 1483–1546) (12 August)

24. Rose of Lima 1586–1617 (24 August)

25. Exaltation of the Holy Cross (14 September)

Autumn to Winter—taking time to be still

October, November, December

26. Martin De Porres 1579–1639 (3 November)

27. Albert the Great, 1206–1280 (15 November)

28. Henri Dominique Lacordaire 1802–1861 (21 November)

29. Catherine of Alexandria 287–305 (24 November)

30. Teresa Chicaba, 1676–1748 (6 December)

31. Antonio de Montesinos 1475–1545 (21 December)

32. Edward Schillebeeckx 1941–2009 (23 December)

33. Advent

34. Christmas

35. Françoise-Catherine (Marguerite Gérine) Fabre 1811–1887 (31 December)

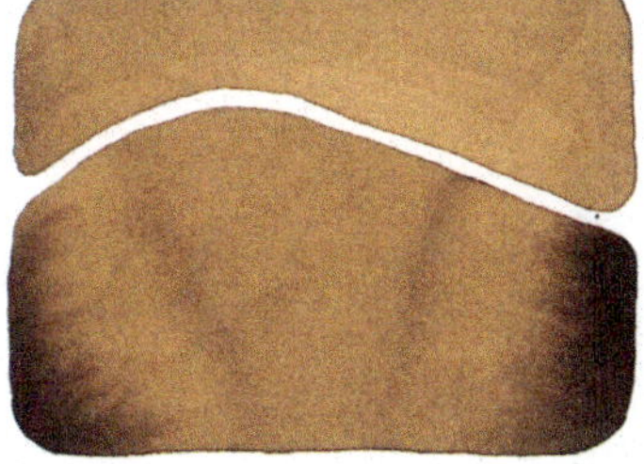

Profound Leaning

Ground of
my being

Discipline of
right relationship

Tree of Life
Source of Love

Intimations of
Presence

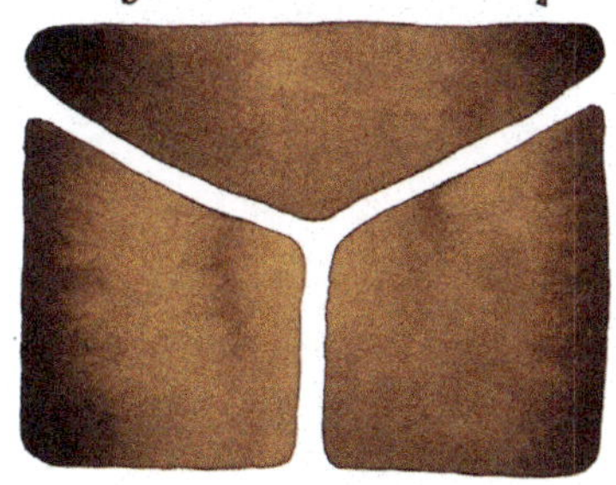

Outstretched

Heart-bound

Open Book

Itinerancy

Preface

Dominican spirituality, as the Cabra Collective notes, defies any attempt to reduce it to a system or type or to set it in concrete so that it's fixed forever. While it has strong roots in the life of St Dominic and the earliest Dominicans, it has depended for the last 800 years on those who have come after them to absorb it and express it in new ways.

This book is one such expression of Dominican spirituality. Grounded in our Australian context and almost 150 years after the first Dominican Sisters arrived in Adelaide, South Australia, from Cabra, Dublin, it draws on a rich tradition yet offers it in an accessible, season-by-season format to meet the needs of contemporary readers. It is not designed to be read from cover to cover in one sitting. Rather, it is offered as a gift for the moment: it is a simple matter to pick up this book and, in its spacious and beautiful pages, to find a saying, a prayer or a fragment from the life of a particular Dominican that provides strength and inspiration for a day, a week or a month. And inspiration can be found not only in the written word but also (and perhaps especially) in the exquisite work of Dominican artists which both provides commentary on the text and at the same time can take us to another place in our reflection.

We can sometimes be tempted to imagine that meaningful prayer or reflection can only happen in the rarefied atmosphere of a retreat when the demands of work and family life can be set aside. But, as our Dominican brother, Erik Borgman, reminds us:

> *Dominicans are convinced that the world in which we live, turbulent and restless, often violent and terrifying, is where we encounter and listen to – 'contemplate' – God.*
> *We may ask what life is all about in the coffee bar or the theatre; we may find the answer to an all-important question or the insight which we have been seeking for so long while telephoning or reading a bedtime story to a child.*[1]

'Freedom and Responsibility' invites its readers to bring the richness of Dominican spirituality into dialogue with their own lived reality and to see the face of God in the events and the people with whom they share this moment in history. This is surely what Dominic himself saw as the heart of the Christian life: to come to know the God at our centre and to bring that God to birth in our world.

Bernadette Kiley OP
CONGREGATION LEADER
HOLY CROSS CONGREGATION, ADELAIDE SA

1 Borgman, *Dominican Spirituality*, 29

Introduction

Freedom and Responsibility

Weaving the Threads of Dominican Spirituality

The Dominican tradition, unlike other religious orders in the Catholic Church, has no collection of writings by its founder, St Dominic (1171–1221), nor any set of spiritual exercises or spiritual writings which can illuminate a 'Dominican way' or a Dominican spirituality. But there are actions, ideas, snippets, thoughts, writings and sayings of wise and holy women and men throughout the ages which we can draw upon to better understand Dominican spirituality.

Dominicans have a long history, dating from Dominic's founding of the first community of women at Prouille in southern France in 1206. Later, in 1214, the first community of friars was established in Toulouse. In December 1216 Pope Honorius approved the establishment of Dominic's plan for an order of contemplative, itinerant preachers.

To try to define Dominican spirituality is problematic. In many ways it is an unnecessary activity, for as will be shown in this volume, Dominican spirituality is a flourishing garden of many blooms. As Catherine of Siena (1347–1380) wrote many centuries ago, Dominic 'made his ship very spacious, gladsome and fragrant, a most delightful garden . . . [in which] the perfect and the not-so-perfect fare well'.[1]

As the Dutch theologian Edward Schillebeeckx explained, Dominican spirituality must begin with an understanding of how Dominic and his first followers responded to being followers of Christ in their own time. Second, because the life, death and resurrection of Jesus provided a critical touchstone for Dominic, as it has for all Christians in all times and places, it is to the story of Jesus that today's Dominicans must look as they seek to give new life to the story of Dominic in their own time. Schillebeeckx argued, in fact, that Dominican spirituality is valid 'only in so far as it takes up the story of Jesus and brings it up to date in its own way'. Third, Dominican spirituality is critically engaged in the world. We cannot be present to God if we are not also present to our own times and to the needs of these times.

This book aims to provide a way of reflecting on the major themes of Dominican spirituality. It can be used as a book of inspiration, contemplation or prayer, or as a resource for beginning an investigation into some of the key figures in the Order's tradition.

1 *Il Dialogo*, chapter 158.

In putting this book together the editors have purposely avoided any of the phrases or mottos traditionally used when describing the Dominican charism, Truth (*veritas*), to praise to bless and to preach (*laudare, benedicere, praedicare*), and to contemplate and to hand on the fruits of contemplation (*contemplari et contemplate aliis tradere*). While each has its rightful place in the tradition, and will be seen to be woven in to the writings and work of many in this book, the editors were seeking something simple and new.[2]

The collection is organised according to the seasons and the months of the year. Each season, as well as significant feast days in the Church's year, provides a selection of writings, biographies or short quotations from Dominican women and men. The written text is enhanced by beautiful art work and photographs produced by Dominicans.

Originally the book was collated with the intention of being a gift from the school for Year 12 students to take with them to read and reflect on at different times in their lives., At the same time, we wanted this to be a unique book, different from other books that are given to students in their final year. We wanted it to be filled with colour and invitation and with free flowing ideas.

2 For more see Donald J Goergen, *St Dominic: The Story of a Preaching Friar* (New York, Mahwah NJ: Paulist Press, 2016).

We wanted one which in some way captured the metaphor of Dominican spirituality as a 'garden' of different blooms. We wanted it to excite, to give pleasure, to be a beautiful book to hold and one to stimulate new ideas based on an ever-deepening dialogue with the Dominican tradition.

In the process of collating this volume, we soon realised that the book had potential, not only as a gift for final year students, but also it could be used by many different people who wish to have a reflective book on the Dominican tradition to use throughout the year and throughout life. If it serves any of these purposes then we have achieved our aim!

Undoubtedly there are many, many women in the tradition who over time have contributed to the garden that we can call Dominican spirituality, but whose voices and writings have not been preserved. This is the sad reality of how women have been, and still are, regarded in hierarchical systems where men and men's ideas are taken as the norm. However, this volume does contain a good representation of writings of contemporary women who have written on themes in both the Christian and Dominican traditions. At least these voices are recorded and will be heard here in this volume. In this way, they will not be lost.

The sources for the quotes in this book are many and varied and where possible they are highlighted and are detailed in the bibliography.

The Cabra Collective

September 2016.

Winter to Spring—seeking justice

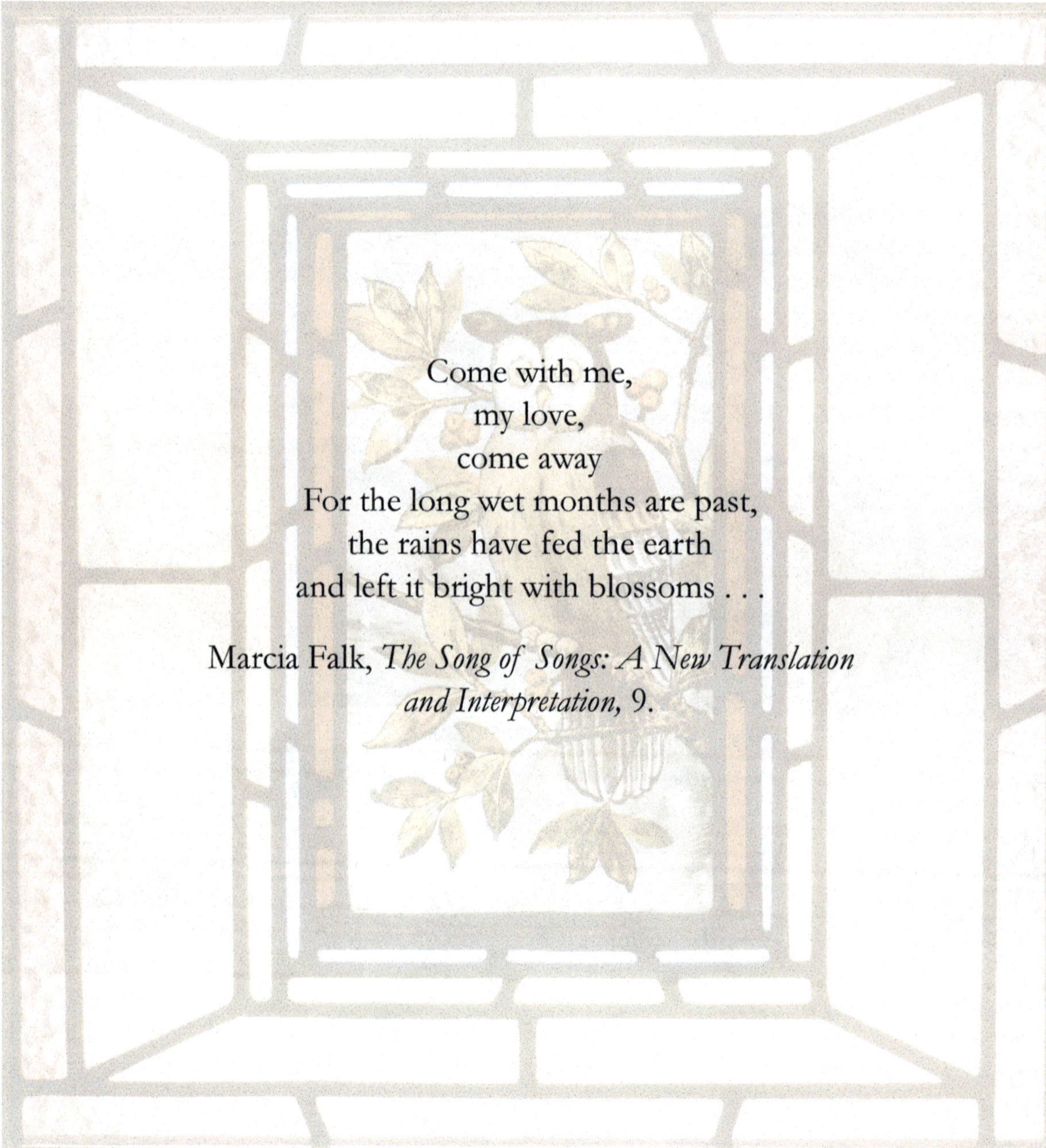

Come with me,
my love,
come away
For the long wet months are past,
the rains have fed the earth
and left it bright with blossoms . . .

Marcia Falk, *The Song of Songs: A New Translation and Interpretation*, 9.

1. Mary, Mother of God 1 January

In Dominican spirituality Mary, the Patron of the Order, is a central figure and the object of much devotion. As a young and vulnerable woman she said yes to the challenging role of being the mother of Jesus of Nazareth. As the first of the disciples she walked with him through his life and remained with him through his suffering and death. She shared the disciples' experience of the fiery transformation of Pentecost. She shows us what it means to 'give birth' to God in our world.

'What good is it to me if Mary is the mother of God if I am not also the mother of God?'
Meister Ekhart

'The Church can no longer forego women's experiences and at the same time remain trustworthy in its proclamation of the good news. Women themselves want to give voice to their world views and not be interpreted through a male lens. We are baptized to be priest, prophet and king, representing Christ to our fellow pilgrims. This has to be translated into practice.'
Madeleine Fredell, OP '"The Apostle to the Apostles": Women Preaching the Good News', 174.

'I think this is what's happening in the Catholic Church at the moment. Women are seeing that our gifts are needed at all levels of the Church—not only at the parish level or in secondary roles. Women have gifts in leadership that are not being used by the Church, and both the Church and women themselves are suffering diminishment as a consequence.'
Trish Madigan OP, 'Traditions and Transformations: Catholic and Muslim Women in Dialogue', 39.

'The reality is I have a voice—a voice strengthened by the communities that have nurtured me, given substance by my education and experience. That I remained unseen or unheard in ecclesial arenas spoke of the institutional Church's blindness and deafness, not of my invisibility or muteness. I had a responsibility to all marginalised people,

and especially women, to find and follow the path by which I might achieve my own freedom and flourishing, and work toward the transformation in the Church's thinking through which women might take their rightful place as equals …'
Kathleen McManus OP, 'Theological Education in the Dominican Tradition: Healing Educating Relationships', 238.

2. Teresa Moore (1840–1873) 14 January

Teresa Moore was the first Prioress of the Dominican community established at St Mary's, Franklin Street, Adelaide. At the age of twenty-three, after having been educated by the Dominican Sisters at Cabra, Dublin, she became a member of their community and was professed in 1863. Five years after her profession, on 9 September 1868, she embarked with six other Dominican Sisters from Cabra on a journey to the other side of the world. The Sisters were responding to a request from Bishop Sheil of Adelaide for Sisters to establish a secondary school for girls in his diocese. The youngest Sister was eighteen and the eldest in her thirties. For much of the time as Prioress of the fledgling community at Franklin Street, Teresa suffered poor health. She died January 14 1873 at the age of thirty-three. She was known to her Dominican community as having 'wise foresight' and her loss was keenly felt by the remaining Sisters.

'Teresa Moore had led a group of young Irish sisters to a foreign land knowing that they would in all probability never see their homeland again . . . they opened their school, St Mary's, Franklin Street, in February 1869, barely two months after their arrival, having completed a building project to accommodate larger numbers of students, planned the forthcoming school year, settled into a new community space, and confronted for the first time the strangeness of colonial life and the unpredictability of local church politics. Twenty pupils were present on opening day, the first enrolment having come from Matilda Solomon, a young Jewish girl, who later became the first lay teacher. There were nine boarders, from both Catholic and Protestant families.

The Sisters offered a curriculum that included grammar, history, geography, astronomy, French, Italian, needlework, writing, arithmetic and the use of the globes. Beneath these facts and figures lie an openness, a breadth of theology, a warmth of welcome and an extraordinary grasp of what constituted excellence in education.'
Bernadette Kiley OP, November 2012, at the opening of the Teresa Moore Centre, Adelaide.

3. Marie Poussepin (1653–1744) 24 January

'Marie Poussepin, born in the French city of Dourdan, was a successful Christian business woman for many years. While still young, she had to take over the family hosiery business, including training apprentices. Marie carried out these duties with efficiency and social sensitivity. The innovations she introduced, adopted by others, raised the socio-economic level of the whole city.

While still in business, Marie, in her thirties, joined the Dominican Tertiaries, a secular group of lay people committed to works of charity. When her younger brother took over the business, Marie, aged forty-two, began her major life work. Moved by compassion for the poor in that region, she sacrificed her assets (retaining capital needed for her foundation) and left Dourdan to found what was then a new form of Dominican religious life: her sisters provided basic schooling and other social services for the poor, but without the usual monastic enclosure. In addition, to ensure the community's financial independence, Marie's sisters earned their own living by making and selling hosiery. Marie died on 24 January 1744. Circumstances have changed today, but her Congregation continues in many parts of the world.'[1]

'… Dominicans can only mediate the story of Jesus effectively by the modelling of their own life. As Blessed Marie Poussepin showed us so clearly, life can preach more powerfully than words.' Lilly Chalakkal OP, 'East Meets West: A Spiritual Journey in Search of New Horizons', 300.

1 Based on Gabrielle Kelly OP, 'Working for Justice and Peace: Glimpses of the Dominican Story', 2015. [Contains references to original sources].

4. Thomas Aquinas (1225–1274) 29 January

Doctor of the Church

Thomas was born near Naples in 1225 or 1226. He was the youngest of many children from a family of the lower nobility. His early years were spent at the Benedictine Abbey of Monte Cassino. He entered the Dominican Order and was sent to Paris for his noviciate and to study philosophy under the Dominican Albert the Great. He became a Master of Theology in 1257, a title awarded to those with exceptional ability in theology. In his teaching and writing Thomas sought to show that human life is the search to know the God of infinite wisdom and love, who creates, sanctifies, and ultimately brings to fulfilment the whole of created reality in and through the life, death and resurrection of Jesus Christ. Thomas taught in Paris and in Naples wrote his *Summa Theologica.* He was canonised by Pope John XXII in 1323, declared a Doctor of the Church in 1567 and in 1880 patron of Catholic universities.

'I can remember my own discovery as a young Dominican that the theology of Thomas Aquinas was thoroughly time-bound and contextual. That did not lead me to reject Thomism. It was an exciting discovery that enabled me to appreciate Thomas all the more. He was a truly original theologian because he tackled the new questions of his age, questions that others had preferred to ignore.' . . . eventually I came to the conclusion that the real value of studying the great theologians of the past was to learn how to go about answering our own faith questions and the questions of our contemporaries. What we learn from Thomas is how to be fearless in raising new questions and being thorough in searching for answers.'
Albert Nolan OP, *Hope in an Age of Despair,* 16.

'He [Thomas Aquinas] was one of the great thinkers of all time, the Dominican, St Thomas Aquinas, who first brought out fully the truth of what has been called "the liveableness of life". His own century—the thirteenth—did not need much encouragement to find real zest in living, but the year 1946, with its atomic bombs and vast experiments in world-wide ranging bombing must, as a modern commentator on the *Summa* of St Thomas has said, find many waverings in their belief in the liveableness of life. The younger pupils may go on with all gay courage of childhood, but the older ones must hide much wondering and fear under an untroubled manner. Even more must this be true in a school where "thinking on the truths placed before you" is encouraged and developed.'
Speech day 1946 by the Cabra Chaplain presenting the annual report on behalf of the Dominican Sisters.

Listening to Thomas Aquinas . . .

'There is nothing on this earth more to be prized than true friendship.'

'The things that we love tell us what we are.'

'Fear is such a powerful emotion for humans that when we allow it to take us over, it drives compassion right out of our hearts.'

'Show yourself to be loveable to everybody, or at least try to do so…'

'Do not heed by whom a thing is said, but rather what is said you should commit to your memory. What you read, set about to understand, verifying what is doubtful.'

'Follow in the footsteps of that blessed Dominic, who, while he yet had life as a fellow-traveller, brought forth and produced foliage, blossom, fruit—useful and wonderful—in God's vineyard. If you shall have followed these steps, you will be able to attain whatsoever you have in mind.'

5. Catherine de Ricci (1522–1590) 13 February

Catherine was born in Florence, Italy. Her mother died when she was four. At an early age she was sent to a school run by Benedictine nuns where her aunt, Luisa de Ricci, was the Abbess. She was a very prayerful person from a very young age. At the age of nine she was scandalised over some bickering between nuns in the monastery and returned home. She later joined a monastery of Dominican nuns and took the name Catherine after the Dominican tertiary, Catherine of Siena.

By the age of thirty she had become prioress, or community leader. As the prioress, de Ricci became an effective and greatly admired administrator. She was an advisor to princes, bishops and cardinals.

De Ricci lived in the convent until her death in 1590, and was canonised by Pope Benedict XIV in 1746.

Listening to Catherine de Ricci . . .

'We must aim more and more at the accomplishment of the divine will: believing with a firm faith that God loves us more than we love ourselves, and takes more care of us then we could take of ourselves.'

CATHERINE DE RICCI
1522 - 1590

6. Fra Angelico (1386/87–1455) 18 February

Fra Angelico was a renowned religious artist, friar and priest. Guido of Vicchio was born in the region of Tuscany in 1386 or 1387 and studied art in Florence while still a young man. Feeling drawn to religious life he entered the Order at the Priory of San Domenico in Fiesole. He served as Prior of San Domenico and shared the fruits of his contemplation through his paintings for the altars at Fiesole and for the convent of San Marco in Florence. He was called to Rome by Pope Eugene IV to decorate two chapels, one in the Basilica of St Peter and one in the Vatican. Pope Nicholas V also commissioned him to decorate his private chapel at the Vatican. His work is also found in the convent of San Domenico in Cortona and the cathedral at Orvieto. On February 18, 1455, he died in Rome at Santa Maria Sopra Minerva and was buried there. The special quality of his painting earned him the title 'Fra Angelico'.

Listening to Fra Angelico . . .

'When singing my praise, don't liken my talents to those of Apelles. Say, rather, that in the name of Christ, I gave all I had to the poor. The deeds that count on Earth are not the ones that count in Heaven.'

FRA ANGELICO
1395-1455

7. Julia Rodzinska (1899–1945) 20 February

Julia Rodzinska was a Polish Dominican Sister who spent many years as a school teacher. During the German Nazi occupation, she continued her ministry, organising clandestine religious education classes. She was arrested on 12 July 1943 and sent to the concentration camp in Stutthof. There, she covertly nursed sick fellow prisoners, mostly Jews. In the midst of the human misery, cruelty and despair of the concentration camp she continued her ministry by sharing with other prisoners a message of faith, hope and love. She contracted typhus and died in 1945, a few days before the camp was liberated. Julia was beatified on 18 June 1999, along with 107 martyrs of the Nazi concentration camps.

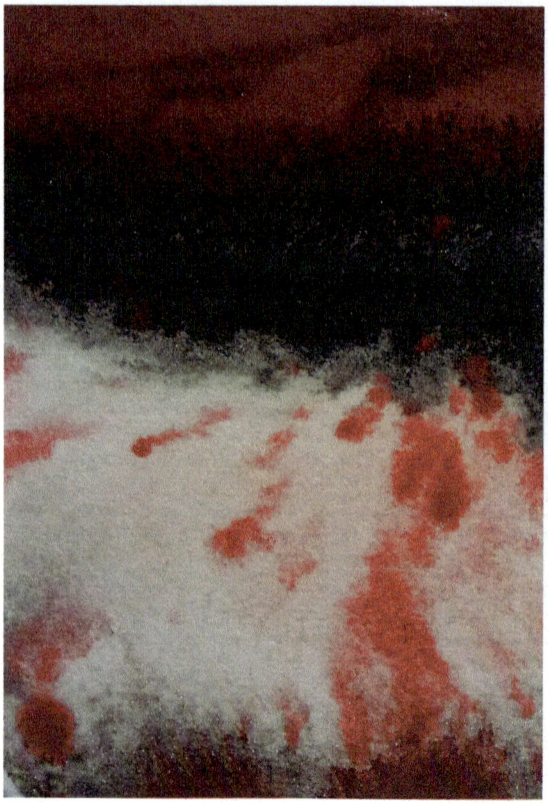

Spring to Summer—celebrating community and diversity

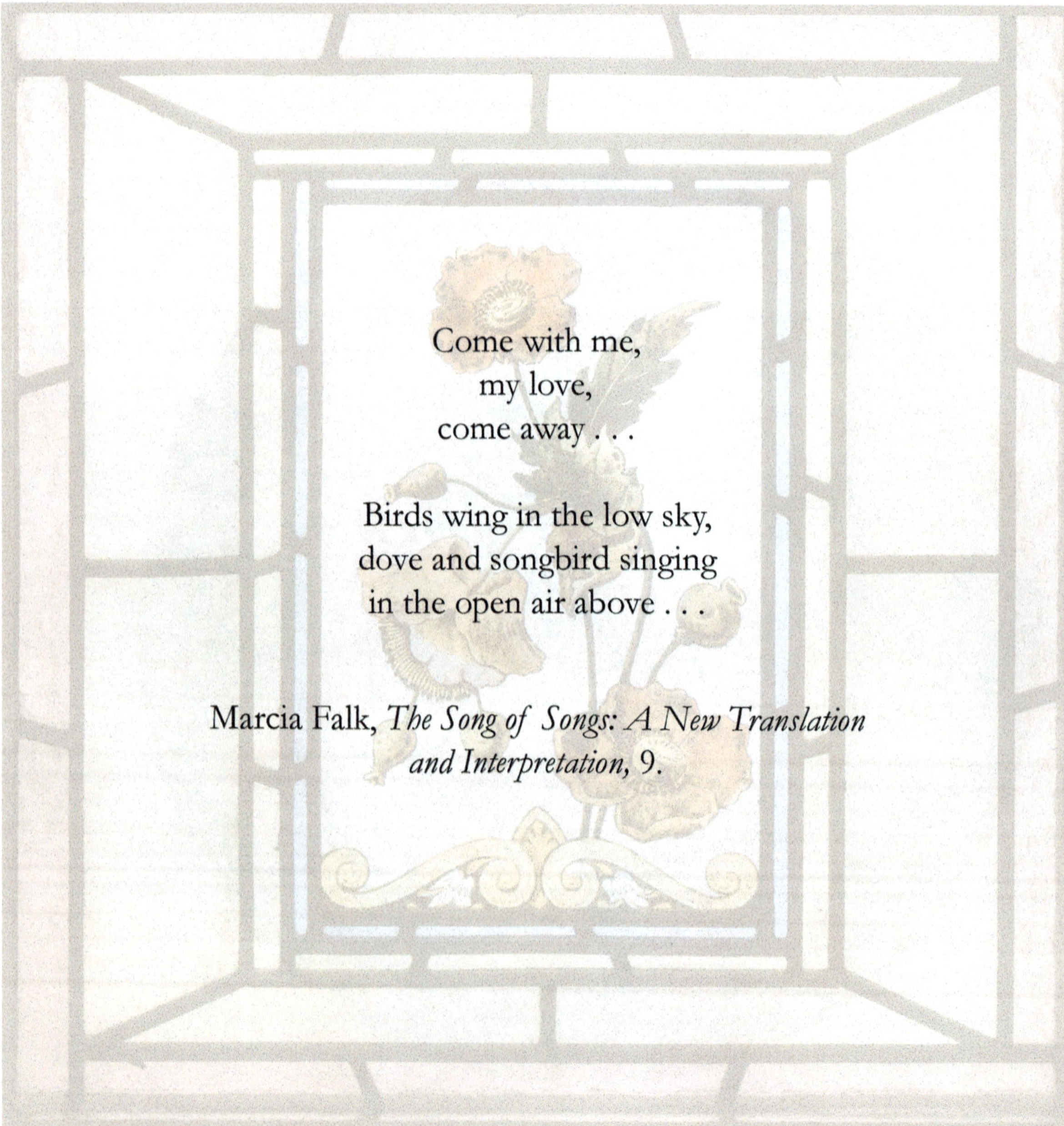

Come with me,
my love,
come away . . .

Birds wing in the low sky,
dove and songbird singing
in the open air above . . .

Marcia Falk, *The Song of Songs: A New Translation and Interpretation*, 9.

8. Margaret of Castello (1287–1320) April 13

Margaret was born blind with severe curvature of the spine, and consequently had difficulty walking.

She was abused, neglected and hidden by her noble parents because they were ashamed of her many physical disabilities. Margaret became a lay Dominican and was greatly loved by the people of Castello, Italy, for her heroic and joyful spirit, her immense charity and her wisdom.

9. Catherine of Siena (1347–1380) 29 April

Doctor of the Church

Catherine was a twin, the twenty-fourth of twenty-five children and was born in the walled city of Siena, Italy. At seven years of age she vowed her life to Christ and at eighteen she became a lay Dominican. It is said she experienced regular mystical experiences and conversations with Christ. At the age of twenty-one Catherine had what she described in her letters as her 'Mystical Marriage' with Christ. Her deep sense of the enduring presence of Christ in her life led her beyond her desire for seclusion and into the lives of the poor and sick of Siena whom she served with extraordinary devotion. Catherine became a prodigious letter writer to princes, church leaders, papal representatives and even the pope, helping to end the Avignon papacy.

When the he pope finally returned to Rome Catherine encouraged him to begin the work of reforming the Church. She died in Rome at the age of thirty-three. She was canonised in 1461. In 1939 she was declared, along with Francis of Assisi, one of the two patron saints of Italy, and in 1970 proclaimed Doctor of the Church. In 1999 she was named as one of the six patron saints of Europe.

Listening to Catherine of Siena . . .

'Be who God meant you to be and you will set the world on fire.'

'Nothing great is ever achieved without much enduring.'

'And the [Creator God] said, "And if anyone should ask me what this soul is, I would say: 'She is another me, made so by the union of love.'

'God eternal, oh boundless love! Your creatures have been wholly kneaded into you and you into us—through creation, through the will's strength, through the fire with which you created us, and through the natural life you gave us.'

'It is the nature of love to love as much as we feel we are loved and to love whatever the one we love loves.'

'It is only through shadows that one comes to know the light.'

'I have put you among your neighbours so you can do for them what you cannot do for me—love them without any concern for thanks and without looking for any profit for yourself. Whatever you do for them I will consider done for me.' Jesus to Catherine of Siena

10. Mother Columba Boylan (1847–1910) 3 May

Columba Boylan arrived in Adelaide in 1875, in the second group of Dominican Sisters to come to Franklin St, Adelaide, South Australia, after the death of the founding Prioress, Teresa Moore. She came as a young religious, having been professed in 1869 in the Dominican community at Cabra, Dublin. The day after her arrival in Adelaide she was appointed as prioress of the Adelaide community. She held this office for six consecutive three year terms and after an interval of three years was prioress for another two terms. Thus for twenty-seven years of her thirty-five years in Australia she 'was a guiding star of her nuns in South Australia.'[1]

Columba Boylan was the first Prioress of Cabra Convent and therefore the first 'Principal' of the school when it opened its doors in 1886. She is remembered both as a wonderful community leader and an exceptional educator:

'Mother M Columba, in character, was indeed true to her name—as gentle as the dove. In the affairs of her community she ruled with so wise and so gentle a sway that the firmness and authority with which these qualities were combined never pressed any way unduly. Her greatest care was for the children in their schools. In the management of the Dominican schools she had always a clearly defined policy, from which no inducement of worldly gain or advantage could tempt her. Brilliant publicity was relegated to a secondary place in comparison with the more solid and lasting requirements which would best serve the pupil in later life … [she] held firmly to her educational ideals and to the community she was never tired of inculcating the importance of educating the hearts as well as the minds of their pupils.'[2]

1 *Golden Jubilee Veritas*, Cabra College, 1918, 11.
2 Obituary from the *Southern Cross*, 13 May 1910.

One of Columba Boylan's first pupils recalled her time at Cabra with much affection:

'After we boarders arrived at Cabra early in 1886, the first familiar figure that greeted us was the statue of Our Lady of the Immaculate Conception which rested safely in its niche on the third storey. The building, consisting of the main front porch and the west wing, was set in large grounds which were at first dusty and covered with grass and weeds . . . In concluding this rather inadequate story of our opening year at Cabra, one rejoices to have been allowed to have the privilege of recounting a few facts concerning school life in those early days. It has been a labour of love, tinged with sadness. Throwing one's memory back over so many decades brings to mind the gaps left in the ranks of our loved teachers and happy school companions. There is no cause to repine, but to offer wholeheartedly a prayer of thanksgiving to God for having raised up so many valiant daughters of St Dominic who have carried his torch with the zeal and vigour of his own days and have firmly implanted in the hearts of thousands of Australians, the great gift of a strong, tenacious and undying faith.'[3]

3 Rose McManus, a foundation boarder at Cabra, in 1911 *Veritas*, reprinted in *Centenary Veritas 1886–1986*, 27.

11. Meister Eckhart (1260–1329) 14 May

Johan Eckhart was born on the River Main in Germany and died in Cologne. He entered the Dominican Priory in Erfurt, in eastern Germany at about the age of eighteen. He studied theology in Cologne and in Paris. Despite a real risk of over simplifying the wonderful teachings of this great 14th century Dominican prophet and teacher, we can surely say Meister Eckhart rejoices in God's presence in all of creation, he encourages us to let go off our attachment to our small understandings, images and language about God. In doing this we create space in our souls and inner selves for the Divine One to be born within us. That is why Eckhart said, 'What good is it to me if Mary is the Mother of God, if I am not also the Mother of God?' As we grow in our sharing of Divinity our transformation is demonstrated in our works of compassion and in our struggle for greater justice for our fellow humans and for all of God's creation.

Listening to Meister Eckhart . . .

'Be sure of this: absolute stillness for as long as possible is best of all for you.'

'You should know that God must act and pour God's self into the moment that God finds you ready.'

'People should not worry as much about what they do but rather about what they are. If they and their ways are good, then their deeds are radiant. We should not think that holiness is based on what we do but rather on what we are, for it is not our works which make us holy but we who make holy our works.'

'Whoever possesses God in their being, has God in a divine manner, and God shines out to them in all things; for them all things taste of God and in all things it is God's image that they see.'

'Since it is God's nature not to be like anyone, we have to come to the state of being nothing in order to enter into the same nature that He is. . .'

'So, when I am able to establish myself in nothing, and nothing in myself, uprooting and casting out what is in me, then I can pass into the naked being of God, which is the naked being of the Spirit.'

'It is a marvelous thing that something flows out yet remains within. That a word flows out yet remains within is certainly marvelous. That all creatures flow out yet remain within is a wonder. What God has given and what he has promised to give is simply marvelous, incomprehensible, unbelievable. And this is as it should be;

for if it were intelligible and believable, it would not be right. God is in all things. The more God is in things, the more God is outside of the things; the more within; the more outside; the more outside, the more within. I have said many times that God creates the whole world right now all at once.'

'We are all meant to be mothers of God . . . for God is always needing to be born.'

'The price of inaction is far greater than the cost of making a mistake.'

'Nobody at any time is cut off from God.'

'The eye through which I see God is the same eye through which God sees me; my eye and God's eye are one eye, one seeing, one knowing, one love.'

'One must learn an inner solitude, wherever one may be.'

'If the only prayer you said in your whole life was "thank you" that would suffice.'

12. LUIGIA TINCANI (1889–1976) 31 MAY

'Luigia Tincani was born in Italy on 25 March 1889. As a young woman, she entered the teaching profession. Luigia felt drawn to Dominican spirituality, sensing in its commitment to the intellectual life and to the evangelisation of culture a charism resonating with her own. After joining the Lay Dominicans in 1909 she recognised a further calling—to dedicate her life entirely to God. Luigia knew of inadequacies in schools and widespread ignorance in matters of faith among university students, so she came to see public schools and universities as her field of missionary activity. She founded a religious community of teachers, formed and sustained by deep prayer and study.

But in the early twentieth century, Luigia felt strongly that a new form of Dominican life, *in* the world, was needed. Her sisters were to live in small groups, working in education, without the distinguishing signs of housing or dress. Her Congregation—Dominican Missionaries of the Schools—was formally established in 1924. Luigia was also a leading figure in promoting new social and professional roles for women in society and church. She decried the fact that there was 'a special vocation from which women were . . . [generally] excluded . . . the intellectual vocation'. In her own life, she became an exemplar of Dominican intellectual life, bringing great breadth and depth of scholarship to all her missionary activity. Luigia died on 31 May 1976 and was declared Venerable in June 2011. Her congregation continues in many countries.'[1]

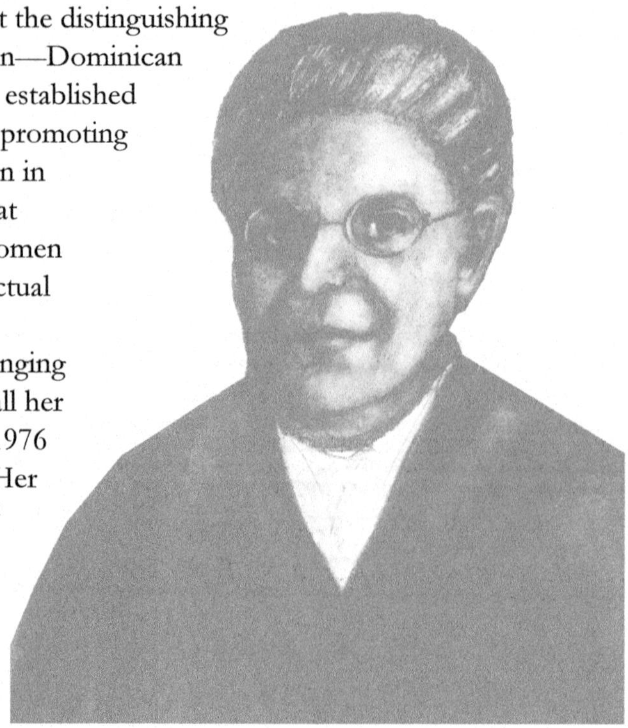

1 Based on Gabrielle Kelly OP, 'Working for Justice and Peace: Glimpses of the Dominican Story' (2015). [Contains references to original sources].

LUIGIA TINCANI
1889 - 1976

13. Segrid Unsedt (1882–1949) 10 June

A novelist of thirty-six books, Segrid was born in Denmark, and her family moved to Norway when she was two years of age. She was one of three children, all girls. Her father died at the age of forty when Segrid was eleven. The family situation meant she did not attend university but worked for ten years from age sixteen in an office. She found time to write at night and on weekends. Her first written piece was published when she was twenty-five. It dealt with adultery in a contemporary world. She left office work after her third novel was published and lived as a writer. She married, Svarstad, a painter, in 1912 and they had three children. Segrid left her husband while expecting her third child in 1919. She grew up as an atheist, converting to Catholicism in 1924 at age forty-two and later became a Lay Dominican. She was awarded the Nobel Prize for Literature in 1928 at the age of forty-six.

In 1940, after the death of her son and daughter and because of her continuing opposition to Nazi Germany, she fled Norway for the USA. She returned in 1945 but undertook no further writing.

Listening to Segrid Unsedt . . .

'In a way we do not want to find the Truth, we prefer to seek and keep our illusions.'

'All my days I have longed equally to travel the right road and to take my own errant path.'

'And when we give each other Christmas gifts in His name, let us remember that He has given us the sun and the moon and the stars, and the earth with its forests and mountains and oceans—and all that lives and moves upon them. He has given us all green things and everything that blossoms and bears fruit and all that we quarrel about and that all we have misused . . .'

'Many a person is given what is intended for another, but no person is given another's fate.'

'No one and nothing can hurt us . . . except what we fear and love.'

'It is a good thing when you don't dare do something if you don't think it's right. But it's not good when you think something is not right because you don't dare do it.'

'Stay calm and do not flee from God who has been seeking you before you even existed in your mother's womb.'

14. Mechtild of Magdeburg (1208–1292/94)

Born in Germany and known as one of the Rhineland Mystics, Mechtild of Magdeburg was a lay woman, a Beguine, who had a strong association with the Dominicans. Heinrich of Halle OP (her confidant) had her book, 'The Flowing Light of the Godhead', published and translated. Mechtild loves a God who is not distant but is vulnerable to pleasure and to pain. God undergoes pain and God rejoices when pain is relieved. God dances with us and we with God.

Listening to Mechtild's four-fold pathway . . .

Delighting
Love flows from God to humans without effort:
as a bird glides through the air without moving its wings . . .

Sinking
Spiritual persons who dwell on earth are offered two kinds of spirit:
in this way two pure natures come together, the first is the flowing fire of the Godhead
and the second is the gradual growth and expansion of the loving soul.

Awakening
Woman! Your soul has slept from childhood on.
Now it is awakened by the light of true love. In this light the soul looks around her to discover who it is who is showing Him/Herself to her here.

Now, she sees clearly
She recognizes for the first time how God is All in All.

Doing
Justice demands that we seek and find the stranger, the broken the prisoner and comfort them and offer them our help. Here lies the holy compassion of God.

from Sue Woodruff, *Meditations with Mechtild of Magdeburg.*

15. The season of Lent

Lent calls us again to justice-love–with ourselves, with God, with other people and with all of creation. It is a time of reflection on our lives and especially on our commitment to being doers of justice in our world.

'Lent is that period of thinking and reflecting before Easter in which 'God's love for humanity has been revealed in a special way in the life, ministry, death and resurrection of Jesus of Nazareth.' Mary Catherine Hilkert OP, *Praxis of Christian Experience*, 44.

' . . . it is no coincidence that Jesus did not die in bed. Jesus was executed as a political criminal and a religious blasphemer as the consequence of his "dangerous preaching".' Mary Catherine Hilkert OP, 'Preaching the Folly of the Cross', 41.

Lent is concerned with conversion: 'Christian conversion always involves a two-fold moment: the turn towards God (which is also a turn toward the human community, toward all of creation and toward one's deepest truth) and a turn away from sin (from living as "people of the lie" as less than fully human).'
Mary Catherine Hilkert OP, *Praxis of Christian Experience*, 45.

We shall not cease from
exploration
And the end of our exploring
Will be to arrive
where we started
And know the place
for the first time.
LITTLE GIDDING
T.S. ELIOT

16. Good Friday and Easter

'Jesus was the victim of an unspeakable crime, but as he was dying he managed to pray for those who persecuted him. "Father forgive them", he prayed, "for they know not what they do".' Albert Nolan OP, *Hope in an Age of Despair*, 124.

'Jesus—hanging there in agony on the cross. He is my neighbour. He represents all human beings. He has identified with all of them.' Albert Nolan OP, *Hope in an Age of Despair,* 122.

'The resurrection of Jesus is unlike any other empirical or historical reality. It offers a bridge between history and eternity. . . In the resurrection, God is revealed as the One who acts in favour of life to others, by raising Jesus who sought faithfully to bring God's life to others, especially to the excluded. God raises Jesus from death as a sign that what Jesus lives and dies for, God's reign, has taken root in history. Thus, Jesus' mission is vindicated through the resurrection and God is proved trustworthy in relation to Jesus. God is faithful. Schillebeeckx says: "God identifies (Godself) with the person of Jesus, just as Jesus identified himself with God".' Helen Bergin OP, 'Edward Schillebeeckx and Eschatology: Engaging with Hope', 91.

'The way Jesus reveals God is a surprising and even shocking one, particularly when one thinks of the crucifixion as an image and likeness of God. Perhaps this shows how mysterious God is and how little we know, particularly when we think we know.' Mark O'Brien OP, *ABC Of Sunday Matters,* A51.

'Christians claim that in the resurrection of Jesus, God's power has been poured forth in the world in a radically new way. The spirit of God holds the future age and its activity in the world, fashioning a new creature, making all things new.'
Mary Catherine Hilkert OP: '"Grace-Optimism": The Spirituality at the Heart of Schillebeeckx's Theology', 125.

'We have to experience God's mercy that moves the tombstone, takes our bodies out of the earth and makes us brothers and sisters, changing us into beggars and witnesses to the truth by allowing the Spirit of God to dance in an environment of listening in these times of spiritual companionship—a companionship that becomes an art—the art of dancing, singing and enlightening.'
Maria Julia Ardito OP, Emmaus Spiritualities Centre: Popular Education and Healing Violence', 212.

17. Pentecost

'To accept history and transform it is part of the following of Jesus and being faithful to his Spirit. We believe that the gospel has been re-enacted in our suburb [in Argentina] through the work of the Holy Spirit, in the actions and words of these women of faith [whom we live and work with], a faith that God is present even in the harshest of realities and most painful moments of life, and in the communities to which these women gave birth, and to which they continue to give life.' Ana Lourdes Suárez and Gabriela Zengarini OP, '"A Mysticism of Open Eyes": Catholic Women's Voices from a Marginal Neighbourhood of Buenos Aires', 140.

'A life in the spirit is a life speaking out about what is wrong in our world, our society, our church and our community; of speaking about the future we are heading for or should be heading for; of speaking out about how God must feel about the events of our time.' Albert Nolan, OP, *Hope in an Age of Despair*, 98.

18. The Eucharist

'In our Eucharistic gatherings we make present again Jesus' gift of self while we also celebrate a foretaste of the eternal feasting, where we will experience perfect oneness with Holy One and with one another'. Barbara Reid OP, *Abiding Word*, 57.

[The Eucharist] 'is a call to us to realise …community by participation in a Christian meal. The living Christ identifies himself with the community at the table, he himself becomes the food and drink that is offered at the meal and we can live in this community . . . ,' Edward Schillebeeckx OP, *The Eucharist*, 125.

[In the Eucharist] '. . . Christ becomes really present in a meal. He gives his death and resurrection as a meal, and this is therefore at the same time…a remembrance,' Edward Schillebeeckx OP, *The Eucharist*, 127.

Summer to Autumn—seeking truth

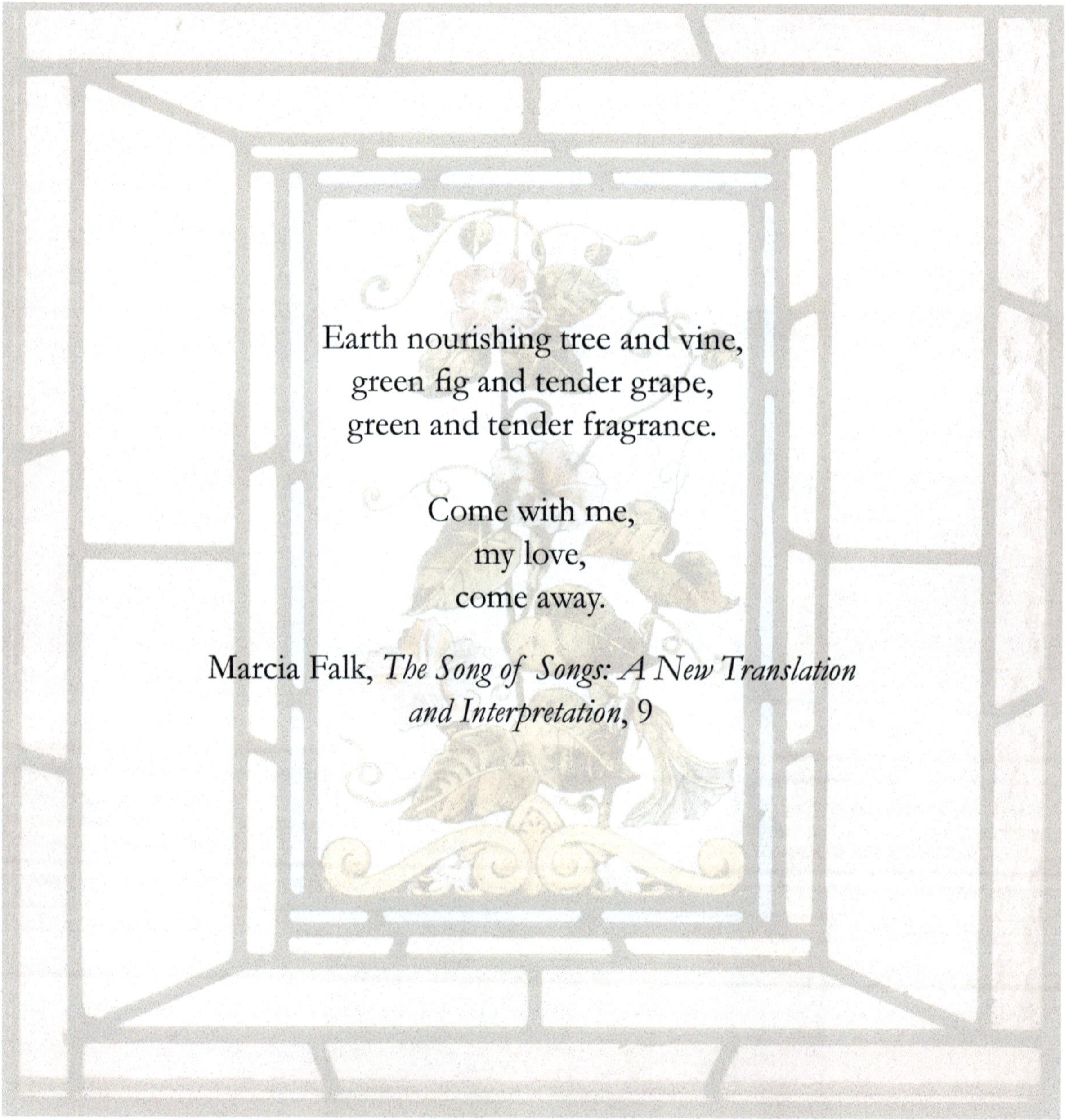

Earth nourishing tree and vine,
green fig and tender grape,
green and tender fragrance.

Come with me,
my love,
come away.

Marcia Falk, *The Song of Songs: A New Translation and Interpretation*, 9

19. Bartolomé de las Casas (1484–1566) 18 July

Defender of the Indians

Bartolomé was born in Seville, Spain in 1484 and died in Madrid in 1566 at the age of eighty-two. His father had accompanied Columbus to the New World in 1493. After four years of study for the priesthood he joined his father in managing a plantation in Hispaniola (now Haiti and the Dominican Republic). He was ordained in Rome in 1507 and returned to Hispaniola in1510. Here, he is said to have heard the sermon by the Dominican Anton Montesinos in 1511 in which he denounced the treatment of the native peoples of Hispaniola by the Spanish.

As a priest, landholder and slave owner, las Casas tried to take Montesinos' words seriously but without making a radical change to his life. He 'pledged himself to two missions—helping the colonists spiritually and making the best profit from colonisation'. This was a promise he could not sustain. Finally, in 1514, las Casas had a conversion after being confronted by a text from the biblical book of Ecclesiastes: 'like one who kills a son before his father's eyes is the person who offers a sacrifice from the property of the poor' (34:24). After his conversion he went with Montesinos to Spain to appeal to the king regarding the treatment of the native peoples. He joined the Dominicans in 1522 and began a life of prolific writing highlighting the plight of his people and the injustices they suffered at the hands of the Spaniards. In 1543 was made Bishop of Chiapas, in today's Mexico.

'Las Casas reminds us that God acts in the midst of humanity and therefore God invites us to act with others.'
Gabriella Zengarini OP, 'Bartolomé de las Casas and Rose of Lima: The Quest for Liberty', 79.

Listening to las Casas . . .

'The pattern established at the outset has remained to this day, and the Spaniards still do nothing save tear the natives to shreds, murder them and inflict upon them untold misery, suffering and distress, tormenting, harrying and persecuting them mercilessly.'

'Those who hear the gospel preached, non Christians especially, must sense that the preachers want no power over them as a result of preaching.'

'Living example: a life visibly virtuous, a life that harms no one, a life blameless from any quarter. A teacher must live his/her own words, must teach by practice more than by presentation. A teacher who talks, only talks, has a rigid effect; in fact is not a teacher but a faker, and two faced. So apostles teach first by deeds, second by words. No need for words when their deeds do the preaching.'

20. Mary Magdalene 22 July

Patron of the Dominican Order

Mary Magdalene is known as the 'Apostle to the Apostles' because of her role in the gospel accounts of the events surrounding the appearances of Jesus after his resurrection.

Mary Magdalene travelled with Jesus as one of his followers. All four gospels include her among those who witnessed Jesus' death and among those who discover his empty tomb. In John's Gospel, she is the first to encounter the risen Jesus and brings word of his resurrection to the other disciples. Unfortunately, she later came to be understood in Western Christianity as a repentant prostitute, even though this is not supported by the canonical gospels.

Mary Magdalene is considered to be a saint by the Catholic, Orthodox, Anglican and Lutheran churches. Other Protestant churches honor her as a heroine of the faith.

As one of the Order's patron's Mary Magdalene is a major figure in the Dominican tradition. She is a contemplative and she is the one who proclaims the news of Jesus' resurrection. She is a powerful and profound image of the preacher, and hence of Dominican life. Her power will be most fully realised when women, including Dominican women, take their place as preachers in the Eucharistic celebration.

How Mary Magdalene came to see Christ 'Having turned around, Mary saw Jesus standing but did not know that it was Jesus, for he did not appear

glorious to her, although the angels saw him as glorious and were honouring him. We see from this that if anyone desires to see Christ, they must turn round to him. Those come to the point of seeing him who entirely turn themselves to him by love.'
Thomas Aquinas from his Commentary on John's Gospel.

'The Gospel of John, which we hear on Easter morning, drives home the central question: where is Jesus now? A single character, Mary Magdalene, represents the voice of the community, as she seeks her beloved, and laments, "We don't know where they have laid him" (20:2). Her search echoes that of the lover in the Song of Songs: "I sought him whom my soul loves; I sought him but found him not" (Song 3:1 [In John's account] on Easter morning, Mary, Peter, and the Beloved Disciple all verify that [Jesus] is not in the tomb. The latter two return home, not understanding, but Mary refuses to leave and continues her search.'
Barbara Reid OP, *Abiding Word*, 37.

21. Jane of Asa (1135–1205) 2 August

Mother of Saint Dominic

Juana de Aza, mother of Dominic, is said to have been born in 1135 in Haza and to have died at Caleruega (Dominic's birthplace) on 4 August 1205. Juana de Aza was beatified in 1828. Tradition has it that she had a dream that she would have a son, who would be a shining light to the Church. While pregnant with Dominic she had another dream in which she saw herself with a dog in her womb holding a burning torch. In the dream, after the dog emerged from her womb, it seemed to set the whole world ablaze.

'In some portrayals the dog with a torch in its mouth seems not to be one running into the world and spreading the fire. It seems, rather, to be offering this torch to Dominic . . . Dominicans find the fire by which they live in the world. They kindle their light at the places where the fire of the divine Spirit burns, resounds in true words and becomes visible in actions which further the true life.'
Eric Borgman, *Dominican Spirituality*, 69.

'Ultimately, the healing and educating of relationships within the Church requires a mysticism of resistance to all that diminishes the contributions of women and thereby jeopardises the Church's viability as a relevant force in the world. The future of the Church depends upon the flourishing of women.'
Kathleen McManus OP, 'Theological Education in the Dominican Tradition: Healing and Educating Relationships', 244.

BL. JANE OF ASA

22. Dominic de Guzman (1171–1221) 8 August

Founder of the Order of Preachers

Dominic was born in Caleruega, Spain in 1171 and died in Bolonga, Italy, in 1221 at the age of fifty-one. At the age of fourteen he began studies in Palencia to prepare for ordination to the priesthood. Even at this young age he showed his sense of responsibility for others by selling his possessions to aid those suffering from a famine. At age twenty he joined a group of priests (canons) attached to the cathedral in Osma. Dominic was ordained a priest at around the age of twenty-five.

In 1203 or 1204 Dominic was sent on a diplomatic mission to Denmark with his bishop, Diego. Travelling through southern France, Dominic witnessed at firsthand the power of the Cathars whose version of Christianity discounted the material world and the physical body, and argued instead for a theology that valued only the 'spiritual'. Dominic and Diego later returned to southern France to preach against the Cathars. They learned from the Cathars that living the simple life of an ordinary person would be of immense help in their efforts to lead people back to a Christianity that avoided the dualistic thinking of the Cathars.

In 1206 at Prouille Dominic founded a refuge for former Cathar women who needed a safe place to live. Some of these women, and those who later joined them, became the first Dominican nuns, and Prouille eventually became the first Dominican convent. He later formed a group of male followers, preachers, and in December 1216 the order was confirmed by Pope Honorius and would be known as the Order of Preachers (OP), or Dominicans.

His small group of preachers were to be different from other orders that existed at the time. Theological education was seen by Dominic to be central, and in 1217 he sent the friars, two by two, to the newly established universities of Bologna and Paris where many became significant teachers of theology. According to Dominic's vision, the friars were not to be bound to one monastery for life, but were to have freedom to move about and preach, were to have no possessions and live a life of radical poverty. Dominic was canonised by Pope Gregory IX in 1534.

'In Dominic's living of Truth he accepted his God-given gifts and used them with gratitude and joy. He acknowledged the intrinsic goodness of all created beings, animate and inanimate, and sought to free people imprisoned in ignorance, irrelevance and ugliness. Through his encouraging love, many moved to a new and joyful acceptance of themselves as worthwhile, and in so doing, found themselves able to bring Christ to others.'
Marie Kerin OP *Veritas*, Cabra College, 1986, 63.

"Perhaps an even more challenging lesson to be learnt from the history of the early years of Prouille is the idea of accepting to be in a process of becoming, which may go on for some time. This necessarily means accepting a degree of fragility, vulnerability. This is how the first sisters of Prouille lived. For what we are to become is rarely fixed at the outset; we become it, we shape it ourselves day by day, in the daily activities that confer meaning on our existences." (Barbara Beaumont OP, *The coming of the preachers*).

Listening to words attributed to Dominic . . .

'I could not bear to prize dead skins, when living skins were starving and in need.'

'Arm yourself with prayer rather than a sword; wear humility rather than fine clothes.'

'These, my much loved ones, are the bequests which I leave to you as my sons and daughters; have charity among yourselves; hold fast to humility; keep a willing poverty.'

'We must sow the seed, not hoard it.'

'You are my companion and must walk with me. For if we hold together no earthly power can withstand us.'

23. Francisco de Vitoria (1483–1546) 12 August

Philosopher, theologian and jurist/lawyer, Francisco de Vitoria was born in Burgos, Spain, in 1483. He was founder of what is known as the Salamanca School, with its focus on just war theory and international law. He joined the Dominicans in 1504 and studied in Paris, teaching theology there for a time until he returned to Valladolid, Spain, where he taught young Dominican friars; many of whom would later go to the New World as missionaries. In 1524 he went to Salamanca, Spain, where he was elected to the Chair of Theology. He died in Salamanca in 1546.

While Francisco never went to the New World as a missionary, much of his life was concerned with issues surrounding Spain's invasion of the newly discovered territories. His writings championed the rights of the native peoples and were deeply critical of the wars waged against them.

He wrote two treatises addressing the problem of Christian states when they 'confront[ed] organized, peaceful non-Christian communities with their own political authority, with their own laws.'

Through his use of the work of Thomas Aquinas he was 'able to think through . . . an order of law binding peoples together in virtue of their common human need for government, freedom of ownership, and pursuit of their lives in communities.'
Roger Rushton, 'Franciso Vitoria: The Rights of Enemies and Strangers', 82.

Listening to Francisco de Vitoria . . .

'After a lifetime of studies and long experience, no business shocks me or embarrasses me more than the corrupt profits and affairs of the Indies.'

'At first sight, it is true, we may readily suppose that, since the affair is in the hands of men both learned and good, everything has been conducted with rectitude and justice. But when we hear subsequently of bloody massacres and of innocent individuals pillaged of their possessions and dominions, there are grounds for doubting the justice of what has been done.'

'If a subject is convinced of the injustice of a war, he/she ought not to serve in it, even on the command of his/her prince. This is clear, for no one can authorise the killing of an innocent person.'

'If such men/women can by examining the cause of the hostility with their advice and authority avert a war which is perhaps unjust, then they are obliged to do so . . . if a person can prevent something which they ought to prevent, and fails to do so, the blame rests with them.'

'Difference of religion cannot be the cause of just war.'

24. Rose of Lima (1586–1617) 24 August

Rose was born in Lima, Peru, in April 1586 and died in August 1617. 'She was a mystic, prophet, contemplative lay Dominican, missionary and theologian. Choosing neither vowed religious life nor marriage, she lived her life as a Christian lay woman understanding her vocation as "God's design". Gabriela Zengarini OP, Bartolomé de las Casas and Rose of Lima: the quest for liberty', 83.

We have very few of her writings, but those that we have can be heard to echo in the writings of Pope Francis. Francis and Rose hold in common the spirit and energy of the people of Latin America who throughout history have often had to struggle against poverty and injustice.

As a child Rose saw the suffering of the Indians subjected to slave labour, and the suffering and the poverty of the women who saw husbands, sons and brothers die. She came to see that her life could be devoted to assisting those who suffered and to encouraging women to work towards a more just society. Rose had the 'mystical daring to see a Church where it is women who prepare the foundation stone of a new Christian community.' Gabriela Zengarini OP, 'Bartolomé de las Casas and Rose of Lima: The Quest for Liberty', 87.

Listening to Rose of Lima . . .

'When we serve the poor and sick we serve Jesus. We must not fail to help our neighbours, because in them we serve Jesus.'

ST. ROSE OF LIMA

25. Exaltation of the Holy Cross 14 September

Eastern Churches, Catholic and Orthodox churches all celebrate the Exaltation of the Holy Cross in September, the anniversary of the dedication of the Basilica of the Holy Sepulchre in Jerusalem.

'We venerate the wood of the cross—exalt it and lift it up—because it was instrumental in the salvation of the world. Of course it is not a piece of wood as such that redeems the world but the love in Christ's heart . . . In a tiny way we experience something of this power of the crucified Christ in our experiences of love. Love always means opening up to the suffering of the one who is loved, sharing it with him or her, and so becoming vulnerable to suffering and pain that is not our own. It is a kind of exposure, it means taking some kind of risk, we leave ourselves open to rejection, perhaps to accusations of not really understanding, to being hurt in one way or another.' Vivian Boland OP, vivianbolandop.blogspot.com. 14 September 2016.

'In a powerful reversal of how human beings see things (a theme that runs throughout the Bible), Jesus prophesies that his own crucifixion, his being lifted up on the cross will become . . . a sign of love and welcome rather than rejection, a sign that attracts rather than repels . . . That transforming power of this love—which from a human point of view looked entirely powerless—is manifest in the transformation of the cross from a hateful and deadly thing into a symbol of love and life.'
Mark O'Brien OP, *The ABC of Sunday Matters*, A175, A176.

'What Christians celebrate is not the cross, nor the sufferings of Jesus, but the power of a love that is faithful even unto death.'
Mary Catherine Hilkert OP, 'Preaching the Folly of the Cross', 42.

INRI
IC
XC
VEN. TERESA CHIKABA
ST. ROSA OF LIMA
WISDOM HAS BUILT HER HOUSE
PROV. 9:1
REV. MO. GERALD BARRY
ST CATHERINE OF SIENA

Autumn to Winter—taking time to be still

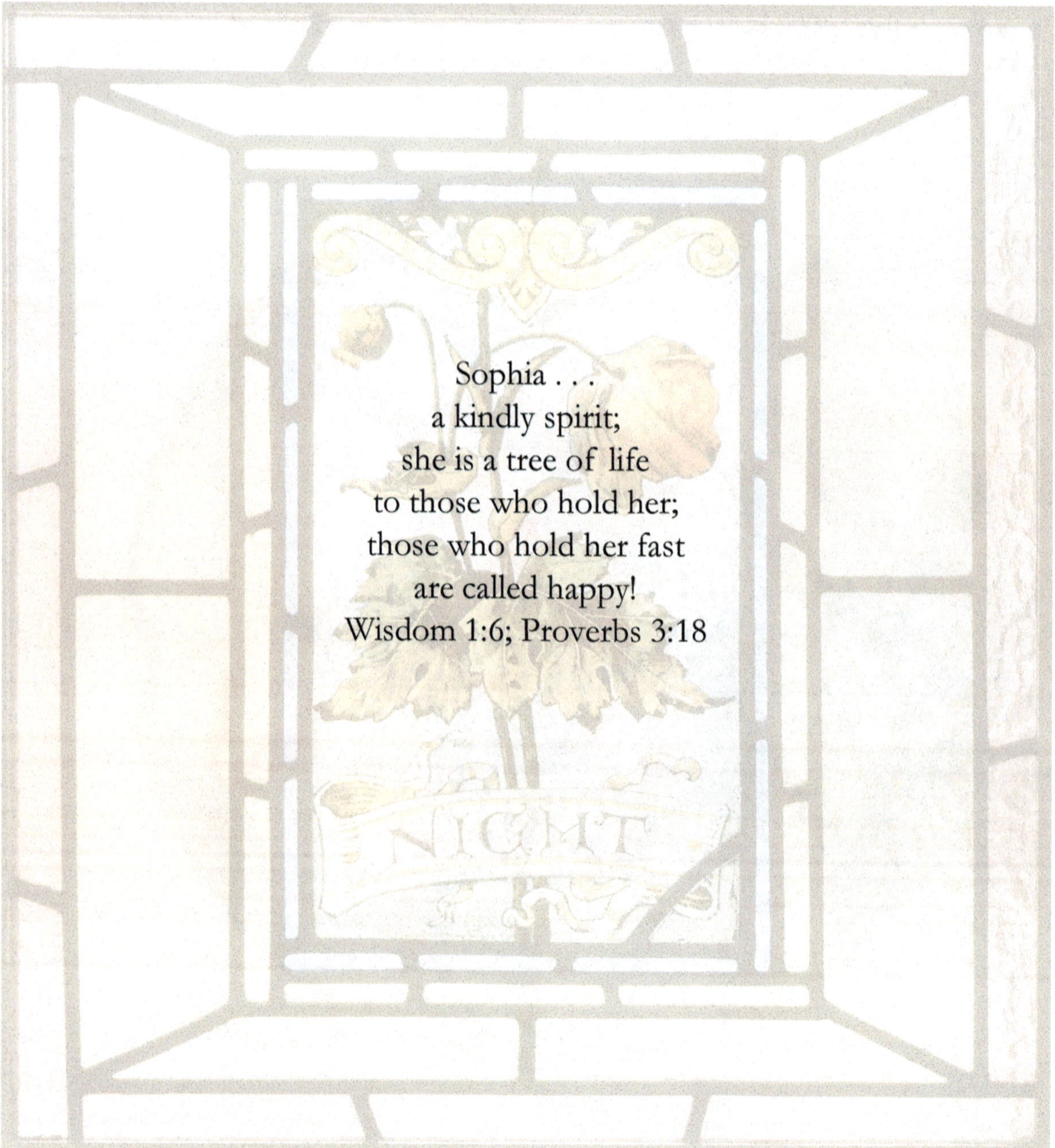

Sophia . . .
a kindly spirit;
she is a tree of life
to those who hold her;
those who hold her fast
are called happy!
Wisdom 1:6; Proverbs 3:18

NIGHT

26. Martin De Porres (1579–1639) 3 November

Patron of Social Justice

Martin was born in Lima, Peru, in 1579. His father was a Spanish nobleman and his mother was a freed slave from Panama. He grew up in poverty after his father abandoned him and his family. Later his father arranged for him to be an apprentice to a barber-surgeon. At fifteen he joined the Dominican community in Lima. He did not become a priest. Rather, his life was devoted to looking after the community and caring for the poor and sick of Lima. He died in 1639 and was canonized in 1962.

Listening to Martin de Porres . . .

'Everything, even sweeping, scraping vegetables, weeding a garden and waiting on the sick could be a prayer, if it were offered to God.'

'Compassion . . . is preferable to cleanliness. Reflect that with a little soap I can easily clean my bed covers, but even with a torrent of tears I would never wash from my soul the stain that my harshness toward the unfortunate would create.'

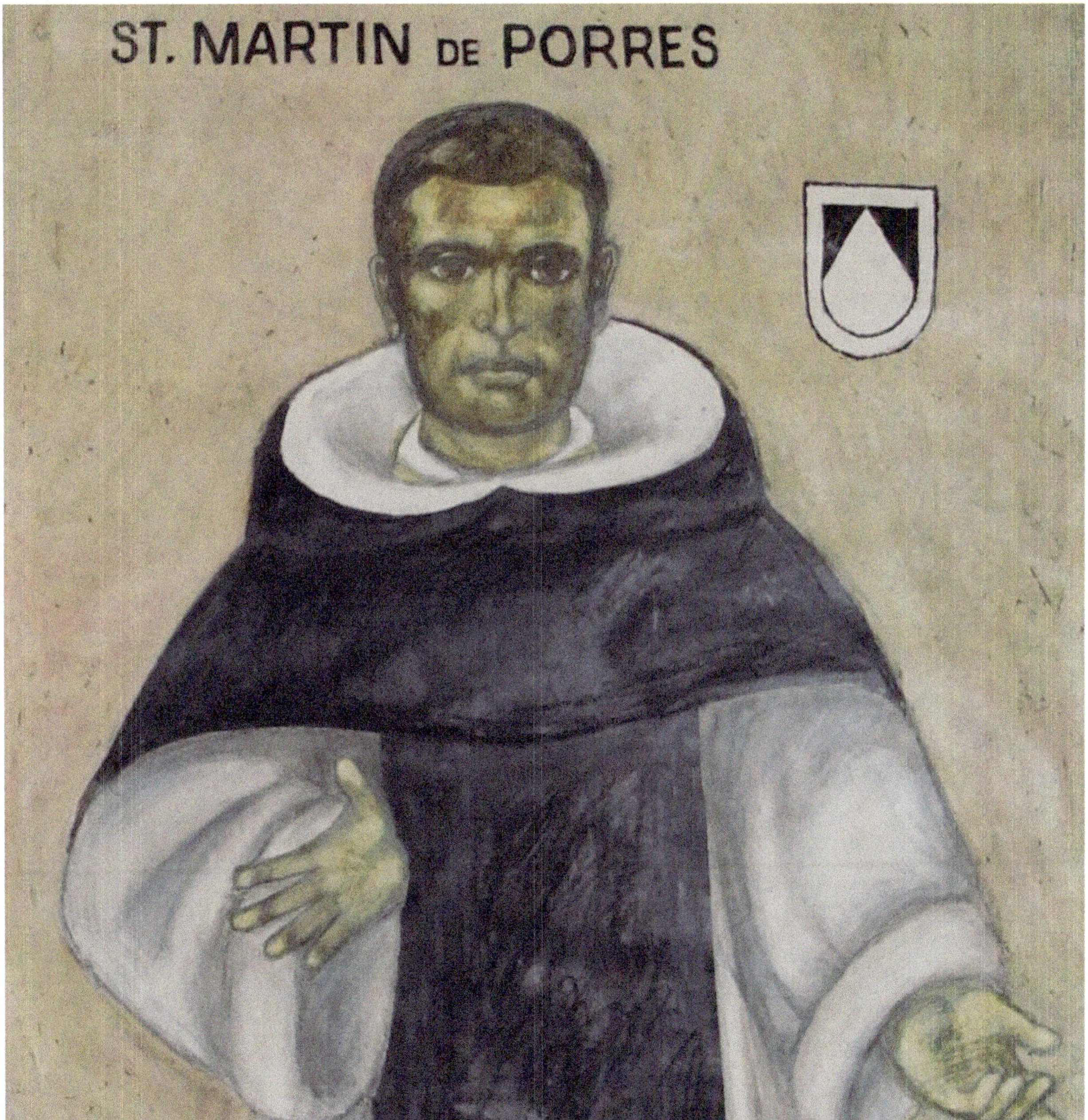
ST. MARTIN DE PORRES

27. Albert the Great (1206–1280) 15 November

Doctor of the Church. Patron of natural scientists.

Albert was born into a knightly family in Germany. He studied in Padua and was interested in theology and the natural sciences. He joined the Dominican Order in Germany and continued his studies. He taught theology in various German cities and then went to Paris to finish his studies. He held the Chair in Theology there from 1245 to 1248. Thomas Aquinas studied with him in Paris and thus began a long collegial relationship between the two.

In 1248 both Albert and Thomas went to Cologne, Germany, to set up a house of study for Dominican friars. He was head of the Dominicans in Germany from 1254 to 1257 and then returned to teaching.

In 1260 he was appointed Bishop of Regensburg in Germany but resigned in 1263. He returned to teaching and was back in Cologne from 1270 to 1277 where he died in 1280. His tomb is just near the Cologne Cathedral.

Listening to Albert the Great . . .

'The aim of natural science is not simply to accept the statements of others, but to investigate the causes that are at work in nature.'

'It is by the path of love, charity, that God draws near the human person and the person to God. But where love, charity, is not found, God cannot dwell.'

'No human science attains this ordering of the universe as perfectly as the judgment of the stars does.'

'In studying nature we have not to inquire how God the Creator may, as God freely wills, make use of human beings to work miracles and thereby show forth God's power; we have rather to inquire what nature . . . can naturally bring to pass.'

ALBERT

28. Jean-Baptiste Lacordaire (1802–1861) 21 November

Henri was a French ecclesiastic, preacher, journalist and political activist. He was born into a family of surgeons and lawyers, and he joined the legal profession. Henri and his brothers gave up the practice of the faith for a time but had a conversion experience after which they returned to the Church. He studied for the priesthood and gave lectures and preached in the Cathedral of Notre Dame in Paris. He joined the Dominican Order in Italy and was part of the re-establishment of the Order in France in the 1840's and 1850's. He was reputed to be the greatest pulpit orator of the nineteenth century.

Listening to Henri Lacordaire . . .

'The universe shows us the life of God, or rather it is in itself the life of God. We behold in it his permanent action, the scene upon which his power is exercised, and in which all his attributes are reflected. God is not out of the universe any more than the universe is out of God.'

'Things go on surviving only because of certain hidden changes which leave the past in the past and proceed into the future by way of harmony with the present.'

29. Catherine of Alexandria (287–305) 24 November.

Protector of the Dominican Order

Saint Catherine was a native of Alexandria, Egypt, a city then famous for its schools of philosophy. She was a daughter of Costis, half-brother of Constantine, and of Sabinella, the Queen of Egypt. Her wisdom and achievements were remarkable, the philosophy of Plato being her favorite study. While Catherine was still young her father died, leaving her heiress to the kingdom. She had a love of study and solitude which displeased her subjects, who desired her to marry, so that her gifts of noble birth, wealth, beauty, and knowledge would be transmitted to her children.

She was both a princess and a noted scholar, who became Christian around the age of fourteen, and converted hundreds of people to Christianity. She was martyred around the age of eighteen.

S. KATHARINA

30. Teresa Chiaba (1676–1748) 6 December

Teresa Juliana de Santo Domingo, was a seventeenth century African and former slave; today honoured with the rank of Venerable by the Church. Kidnapped at the age of nine from her family in Africa and sold into slavery in Spain, Teresa was eventually granted freedom by her owners and entered religious life in a Dominican monastery in Salamanca.

Her marginal status and poor treatment by her religious sisters, coupled with her experience as an African woman to whom polygamy would have been familiar, are all reflected in her anguished experience of spousal mysticism and expressed in her poetry. Teresa is jealous of her divine spouse, Christ, and does not take kindly to having to share him with her sisters. She boldly expresses her unease over this in her poetry, a verse of which she shares with us on the scroll she unrolls for us to read: 'Oh Jesus, what will I say? If you go off with other women, what will I do?'

31. Antonio de Montesinos (1475–1545) 21 December

Antonio de Montesinos became a Dominican at the convent of St Stephen in Salamanca, where he may have studied under Francisco de Vitoria. He was part of the first band of Dominican missionaries to go to Hispaniola Island, in September 1510, under the leadership of Pedro de Córdoba.

With the backing of de Cordoba, and his Dominican community at Santo Dominigo, Montesinos preached against the enslavement and harsh treatment of the Indigenous peoples of the island by the Spanish. Montesinos' preaching led eventually to Bartolomé de las Casas' conversion and his entering the Dominican Order.

Listening to Montesinos . . .

'Tell me by what right of justice do you hold these Indians in such a cruel and horrible servitude? On what authority have you waged such detestable wars against these people who dwelt quietly and peacefully on their own lands? Wars in which you have destroyed such an infinite number of them by homicides and slaughters never heard of before. Why do you keep them so oppressed and exhausted, without giving them enough to eat or curing them of the sicknesses they incur from the excessive labour you give them, and they die, or rather you kill them, in order to extract and acquire gold every day.'

32. Edward Schillebeeckx (1914–2009) 23 December

Edward who was born in Antwerp in 1914 was the sixth of fourteen children. His father was an accountant in the Public Records Office in Belgium. His older brother joined the Jesuits and Edward the Dominicans. His main interest was theology, through which he sought to explore the mystery of God and the Christian response to the critical social questions of his time. He was ordained in 1941 and for most of his life taught theology in Holland, where he died in 2009. He was an advisor to the Dutch bishops during the Second Vatican Council.

Listening to Edward Schillebeeckx . . .

'It is essential for Dominican spirituality to attend to God as God has already revealed God's self to us in the past and to attend to the present-day "signs of the time" in which the same God, who is faithful to us, makes an appeal. Any one-sidedness—in one-track, uncritical judgment either of the past or of what might prove to be symptoms of the future in the present—is un-Dominican. ...'
Schillebeeckx, Edward OP , 'Dominican Spirituality', 105.

33. Advent—Perceiving God-with-us.

'. . . in Advent we call to mind again that divine power is revealed not in pyrotechnic displays of fire and quaking mountains but in the immense love that comes in the form a vulnerable child. God has ruptured the dividing line between divinity and humanity by taking on human flesh in Christ. Advent asks us, likewise, to both embody Christ and to watch for his presence in each one we meet, particularly those who are most needy.' Barbara Reid OP, *Abiding Word*, 2.

Remembering: 'The ultimate claim of Jesus' life, ministry and death was that the compassion of God is the power at the heart of human history and of the universe—the reign of God is at hand.'
Mary Catherine Hilkert OP, '"Grace-Optimism": The Spirituality at the Heart of Schillebeeckx's Theology'.

Autumn to Winter—taking time to be still

34. Christmas

'In our celebration of Christmas we not only rejoice in God tenting with us in human form but as followers of Christ we too are invited out of our comfortable abodes to pitch our tent with the most vulnerable and needy . . .'
Barbara Reid OP, *Abiding Word*, 13.

'The mystery of [God's birth] in the incarnation means God's word will be accomplished in and through human words and human lives.'
Mary Catherine Hilkert OP, *Naming Grace*, 68.

'In view of the incarnation, the word of God is not only promised and announced it is also enfleshed. The word has been entrusted not to privileged individuals but to the Christian community as a whole . . . '
Mary Catherine Hilkert OP, *Naming Grace*, 184.

35. Françoise-Catherine (Marguerite Gérine) Fabre (1811–1887) 31 December

'"Truth and mercy are the key words of Dominican life . . .", as modelled in the life of Dominic.[1] The charism of mercy was outstandingly manifested in Françoise-Catherine. Born in southern France, she was no stranger to hardship. During her youth, Françoise-Catherine's faith and sense of compassion grew stronger. At nineteen, she became a lay Dominican. She was thus able to deepen her knowledge of Dominican spirituality and, with other lay Dominicans, engaged in works of mercy. At the age of thirty-one, Françoise-Catherine dedicated her life entirely to God, forming a new Dominican community of 'home nurses' to tend sick and dying people. At that time, she took the name 'Marguerite Gérine'. The new community, soon adding education to their work, spread rapidly in France, Italy and South America, and today the sisters are found on nearly every continent.'[2]

1 Fr Vincent de Couesnongle, OP, Master of the Dominican Order (1975–84), various talks, including *Confidence for the Future—Addresses to Dominicans* (Dublin: Dominican Publications 1982; talk to Dominican Leadership Conference, United States of America, 22 November 1975.

2 Based on Gabrielle Kelly OP, 'Working for Justice and Peace: Glimpses of the Dominican Story' (2015). [Contains references to original sources].

CERINE FABRE
1811 - 1887

Bibliography

CABRA CELEBRATES

WEAVING THE THREADS OF DOMINICAN SPIRITUALITY

Bergin, Helen F OP, 'Edward Schillebeeckx and Eschatology: Engaging with Hope', in *From North to South: Southern Scholars Engage with Edward Schillebeeckx*, edited by Helen F Bergin OP (Adelaide, South Australia: ATF Theology, 2013), 85–102.

Bergin, Helen F OP, editor, *From North to South: Southern Scholars Engage with Edward Schillebeeckx* (Adelaide, South Australia: ATF Theology, 2013).

Boland, Vivian OP, vivianbolandop.blogspot.com. 'Exaltation of the Holy Cross', 14 September 2016.

Borgman, Eric, *Dominican Spirituality* (London: Contiuum, 2001).

Catholic Women Speak Network, *Catholic Women Speak: Bringing our Gifts to the Table* (New York: Paulist Press, 2015).

Chalakkal, Lilly OP, 'East Meets West: A Spiritual Journey in Search of New Horizons', in *Dominican Approaches to Education*, second edition, edited by Gabrielle Kelly OP and Kevin Saunders OP (Adelaide, South Australia: ATF Theology, 2014), 297–304.

Congar, Yves M-J OP, *Theologians Today: Yves M-J Congar* (London and New York: Sheed and Ward, 1972).

Congar, Yves M-J OP, 'Holy Spirit and Spirit of Freedom', in Congar, Yves M-J OP, *Theologians Today: Yves M-J Congar* (London and New York: Sheed and Ward, 1972), 9–46.

Curtis, Robert, *Dominicana: A Guide for Inquirers,* second edition (Raleigh, North Carolina: Lulu Press, 2004).

de Menibus Jean-Marie OP, 'A Contemplative Listen and Teaches', translated by Patricia Davis OP, in *Dominican Approaches to Education*, second edition, edited by Gabrielle Kelly OP and Kevin Saunders OP (Adelaide, South Australia: ATF Theology, 2014), 99–102.

de Oliviera, Carlos Josephat Pinto OP, 'Las Casas: Educator for Life and Liberation', translated by Maria Marily de Oliveira assisted by Sandra Camilo Ede OP and Hilary Regan, in *Dominican Approaches to Education*, second edition, edited by Gabrielle Kelly OP and Kevin Saunders OP (Adelaide, South Australia: ATF Theology, 2014), 63–74.

Falk, Marcia, *The Song of Songs: A New Translation and Interpretation* (Harper Collins, 1990).

Noffke, Suzanne OP, 'Catherine of Siena: Disciple—Teacher', in *Dominican Approaches to Education*, second edition, edited by Gabrielle Kelly OP and Kevin Saunders OP (Adelaide, South Australia: ATF Theology, 2014), 53–61.

Nolan, Albert OP, *Hope in an Age of Despair* (New York: Orbis, 2009).

Northey, Helen OP, *Living The Truth: The Dominican Sisters in South Australia, 1868–1958*, Dominican Sisters Holy Cross Congregation, 1999.

Hilkert, Mary Catherine OP, '"Grace-Optimism": The Spirituality at the Heart of Schillebeeckx's Theology', in *Spirituality Today*, 44/3 (1991): 220–239.

Hilkert, Mary Catherine OP, *Naming Grace: Preaching and the Sacramental Imagination* (New York: Continuum, 1997).

Hilkert, Mary Catherine OP, 'Preaching the Folly of the Cross', *Word and World*, 19/1 (Winter 1999) 40–48.

Hilkert, Mary Catherine OP, editor, and Schreiter, Robert CPPS, editor, *The Praxis of Christian Experience: An Introduction to the Theology of Edward Schillebeeckx* (San Francisco: Harper and Row, 1989).

Hinnebusch, William, *Dominican Spirituality: Principles and Practices* (Eugene, Oregon: Wipf and Stock, 2015).

Kelly, Gabrielle OP and Saunders, Kevin OP, editors, second edition *Dominican Approaches to Education* (Adelaide, South Australia: ATF Theology, 2014).

McManus, Kathleen OP, 'Theological Education in the Dominican Tradition: Healing and Educating Relationships', in *Dominican Approaches to Education*, second edition, edited by Gabrielle Kelly OP and Kevin Saunders OP (Adelaide, South Australia: ATF Theology, 2014), 235–245.

Mills, John Orme OP, editor, *Justice, Peace and Dominicans 1216–2001* (Dublin: Dominican Publications, 2001).

Murray, Paul OP, *The New Wine of Dominican Spirituality: A Drink Called* Happiness (London: Burns and Oates, 2006).

Nolan, Albert OP, *Hope in an Age of Despair* (Maryknoll, New York: Orbis, 2010).

O'Brien, Mark OP, *The ABC of Sunday Matters* (Adelaide, South Australia: ATF Theology, 2013).

O'Meara, Thomas F OP and Philibert, Paul OP, *Scanning the Signs of the Times: French Dominicans in the Twentieth Century* (Adelaide, South Australia: ATF Theology, 2013).

Reid, Barbara OP, *Abiding Word: Sunday Reflections for Year C* (Collegeville MN: Liturgical Press, 2012).

Rushton, Roger, 'Francisco Vitoria: The Rights of Enemies and Strangers', in *Justice, Peace, and Dominicans 1216–2001*, edited by John Orme Mills OP (Dublin: Dominican Publications, 2001).

Schillebeeckx, Edward OP, 'Dominican Spirituality', in Erik Borgman, *Dominican Spirituality* (London: Continuum, 2001).

Schillebbeeckx Edward OP, *Mary, Mother of Redemption* (London: Sheed and Ward, 1964).

Schillebbeeckx Edward OP, *The Eucharist* (London: Sheed and Ward, 1968).

Vergauwen, Guido OP, 'The Charism of Study in the Education of Dominicans', in *Dominican Approaches to Education*, second edition, edited by Gabrielle Kelly OP and Kevin Saunders OP (Adelaide, South Australia: ATF Theology, 2014), 89–98.

Woodruff, Sue, *Meditations with Mechtild of Magdeburg* (Santa Fe: Bear and Co, 1982).

Zengarini, Gabriela OP, 'Bartolomé de las Casas and Rose of Lima: The Quest for Liberty', translated by Mary Ann Connolly, in *Dominican Approaches to Education*, second edition, edited by Gabrielle Kelly OP and Kevin Saunders OP (Adelaide, South Australia: ATF Theology, 2014), 75 –87.

Appendix 1

Image Credits

page 5	Stained Glass, Cabra Chapel, Adelaide, DON BRICE
page 6	Stained Glass, Cabra Chapel, Adelaide, DON BRICE
page 7	Stained Glass, Cabra Chapel, Adelaide, DON BRICE
page 8	Stained Glass, Cabra Chapel, Adelaide, DON BRICE
page 9	Nine Paths of Prayer, Sheila Flynn OP
page 10	Dominican Education Australia, logo.
page 11	St Dominic Caleruega, Spain
page 12	Prouilhe, Maurice Keating OP, San Sisto College, Brisbane.
page 13	Prouilhe Chapel, Rosemary Yelland OP, DON BRICE
page 14	St Dominic, Stained Glass, Cabra Chapel, Adelaide, DON BRICE
page 15	Stained Glass, Cabra Dominican College, Adelaide, DON BRICE
page 17	Kim En Jong OP
page 19	Stained Glass, Cabra Chapel, Adelaide, DON BRICE
page 20	Madonna, artist unknown, Cabra Chapel, Adelaide, DON BRICE
page 21	The Solomon's Madonna Mother and Child, Rosemary Yelland OP, DON BRICE
page 23	Left, Dominican Sisters, c 1880, Cabra Holy Cross Congregation Archives, Adelaide
page 23	Right, Teresa Moore OP, Cabra Holy Cross Congregation Archives, Adelaide
page 25	Wise Woman 5, Mary Horn OP
page 26	Aquinas, Maurice Keating OP, San Sisto College, Brisbane
page 27	St Thomas Aquinas, Maurice Keating OP
page 28	Wise Woman 4, Mary Horn OP
page 29	Catherine De Ricci, Maurice Keating OP
page 30	Fra Angelico, Maurice Keating OP, San Sisto College, Brisbane
page 31	Fra Angelico, Maurice Keating OP
page 32	Left, Gospel Seepage 4, Sheila Flynn OP
page 32	Right, Bl Julia Rodziinska, Maurice Keating Op
page 33	Wise Woman 11, Mary Horn OP
page 35	Kim En Jong OP
page 37	Stained Glass, Cabra Chapel, Adelaide, DON BRICE

Appendix 2

THE LAST SUPPER - MOVING COUNTER CLOCKWISE FROM CENTRE:
Jesus: He wears a prayer shawl, which Orthodox Jewish men still wear today for prayer on particular occasions.

Mary Magdalene: Mary Magdalene is present as Apostle to the Apostles, the title by which she has been known for most of Christian history in the Eastern Churches; the first to preach the resurrection to her brothers and therefore the first preacher of the Gospel. The Dominicans on her side of the painting in some way express this active, ministerial dimension of the act of preaching.

Bartolomé de las Casas: His writing and activism in defense of the indigenous peoples of the Americas helped bring about reforms of Spanish imperial law. His preaching, writing and activism became part of a centuries-long and highly contentious moral, theological, and legal debate among Dominicans in Salamanca that in time resulted in the emergence of modern international law.

Luis de Cáncer: His passion and commitment to peacefully preaching the Gospel and respecting the cultures and languages of native peoples led to his martyrdom and that of his companions in Tampa Bay, Florida in 1549. He and his companions are the first Dominican martyrs in North America.

Luis Beltrán (or Louis Bertrand): Like las Casas and Cancer, he left Spain to dedicate much of his life to missionary work in the Americas, and he is also the patron saint of novice masters, due his many years serving in that ministry.

Martín de Porres: The patron saint of our province, the cooperator brother Martin de Porres, born in Lima, Peru to a former slave from Panama and a Spanish nobleman. Known for his heroic care for the poor, the sick and the marginalized, Martin was revered and respected during his lifetime as a healer.

Catherine of Siena: Mystic, straight-talking advisor to popes, and Doctor of the Church. Here, Catherine listens silently for what the Spirit would have her commit to her as yet blank page.

Fra Angelico: The famous Florentine artist John of Fiesole, who some have called the last medieval painter and the first painter of the renaissance. Fra Aneglico's portrait of the Virgin is a mirror in which the painter sees himself.

Rose of Lima: Dominican laywoman and mystic, and friend of Martin de Porres.

Teresa Chicaba: Teresa Juliana de Santo Domingo, a seventeenth century African nun and former slave; today honored with the rank of Venerable by the Church. Kidnapped at the age of nine from her family in Africa and sold into slavery in Spain, Teresa was eventually granted freedom by her owners and entered religious life in a Dominican monastery in Salamanca. Her marginal status and poor treatment by her religious sisters, coupled with her experience as an African woman to who polygamy would have been familiar.

Margaret of Castello: Abused, neglected and later exposed by her noble parents because they were ashamed of her many physical disabilities, Margaret became a lay Dominican and was greatly loved by the people of Castello, Italy for her heroic and joyful spirit, her immense charity and her wisdom.

Lorenzo Ruiz: Husband, parent, and lay Dominican. Born in the Philippines to a native Filipina mother and a Chinese father, Ruiz was multilingual and did much translation work for the friars. When he was falsely accused of a crime the Dominicans, who believed in his innocence, found a way for him to leave the *Philippines as a missionary.* He was supposed to go on a mission to China but was mistakenly sent to Japan instead, during a particularly cruel persecution of Christians there. Ruiz was captured and brutally tortured for a year, eventually dying at the hands of his torturers.

Catherine of Alexandria: Catherine represents the centrality of contemplative study to preaching and the Dominican way of life. She sets aside Greek scroll with a verse from the Book of Sirach that she has been studying, a Scripture proclaiming that before the world was formed, Wisdom was. She puts the scroll aside to gaze directly at Wisdom in Person. The figures on Catherine's side of the table are depicted in such a way that they visibly express various dimensions of the life of prayer and /or study.

Cristóbal Torres OP

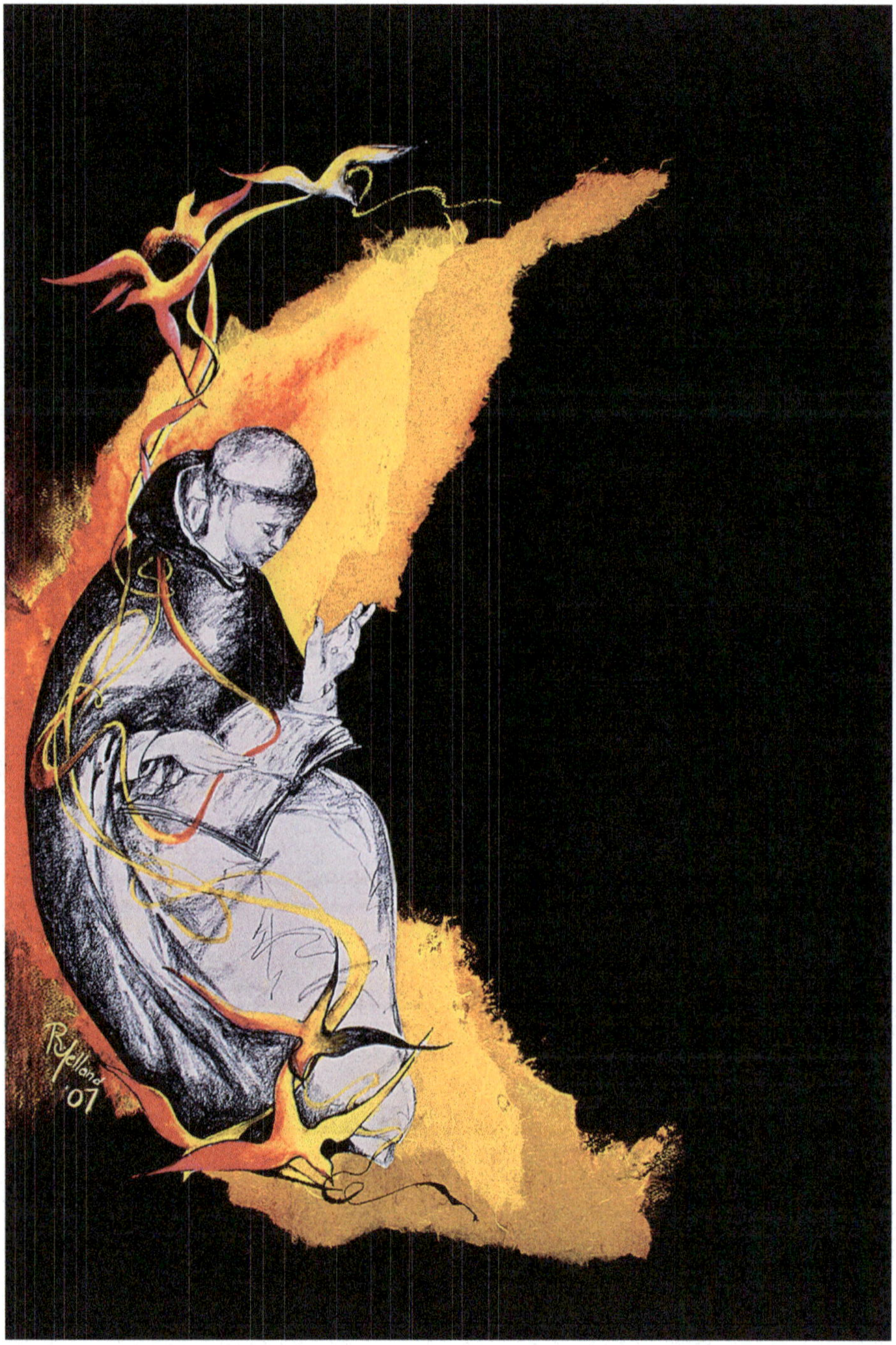
R Yelland
'07

CPSIA information can be obtained
at www.ICGtesting.com
Printed in the USA
BVOW05*1946060417
479647BV00018B/13/P

9 781925 309546